I dedicate this book to parents and grandparents everywhere.
Theirs is the most precious and important of responsibilities.

Also, to Charlie and Lilibeth.

Tom Malone

WHAT ARE YOUR CHILDREN WATCHING?

AUSTIN MACAULEY PUBLISHERS™

LONDON • CAMBRIDGE • NEW YORK • SHARJAH

A CIP catalogue record for this title is available from the British Library.

ISBN 9781528947053 (Paperback)
ISBN 9781528947060 (Hardback)
ISBN 9781528972079 (ePub e-book)

www.austinmacauley.com

First Published (2019)
Austin Macauley Publishers Ltd
25 Canada Square
Canary Wharf
London
E14 5LQ

Table of Contents

Introduction

My purpose in writing this short book is to express my extreme concern and to raise an alarm regarding what I personally consider to be a virtual and unprecedented tsunami of potential damage, hurt and harm awaiting our children and young people if the rushing flood of today's highly politicised and sexualised culture is continued to be allowed to saturate their young minds.

All generations that have gone before, whilst having their own diverse problems and challenges, have innately, intuitively, naturally and intentionally, guarded and protected their young – guarded them from some of the realities of life until they were sufficiently grown to deal with them; guarded them from some of the 'facts of life' until they were sufficiently mature enough to understand them.

But today, new government guidelines and legislation for primary school curriculums regarding sexual and 'relationship education' are being proposed that threaten to dilute, undermine and eventually eradicate that protection. Thereby exposing our young children to adult-themed information, which can only cause them irrevocable harm.

Children and young people are also being exposed to unfiltered, unregulated and uncensored materials and influences via the internet and social media platforms. Evidence is emerging throughout society every day of the corrosive, corruptive and damaging effects of this media.

My hope is that parents and grandparents (the real experts on what is best for their children) will take notice, take stock and take action!

Personal Profile

The author served as a professional social work practitioner with the local authority for 28 years. As a team manager for almost 20 of those years, he specialised in Crisis Intervention and Children and Families work with specific emphasis on Statutory Child Protection.

He was also an Accredited Mental Health Officer. In a voluntary capacity he has also worked extensively with young people, most recently pioneering a major youth music initiative in collaboration with the Scottish Arts Council (now Creative Scotland) and a host of other statutory and private sector organisations.

After retiring from social work practice in 2011, he served a 5-year term as a local authority councillor. In addition to serving on a number of committees and dealing with wide-ranging constituency matters, his focus was on environmental and economic regeneration.

He has therefore gained considerable knowledge and experience in working very closely with vulnerable and at-risk individuals and diverse groups of people across the social spectrum in both statutory and voluntary sectors. He maintains a passion for striving for the best possible opportunities for children, young people and their families.

Chapter 1
Setting the Scene

We live in a breathtakingly fast and ever developing technological age. In addition to the internet, new information media, social media platforms and apps appear on a regular basis. Seemingly limitless information is evermore available to us, quite literally at our fingertips.

Instant and immediate information, visuals and images of every conceivable kind are available to us, anywhere and at any time, twenty-four hours a day, seven days a week, three hundred and sixty-five days a year.

Anything – think about that for a minute, anything and everything is instantly and immediately, loaded and ready to go. All that the world has to offer. From absolutely anywhere. From absolutely anyone. Saying and displaying absolutely anything. All freely and instantly accessible by anyone – by the mere tap of a keypad or a touchscreen. And accessible by our children and youngsters.

Therefore, it is increasingly important for us all to acknowledge and recognise the influences and pressures, particularly affecting children and young people today from all aspects of the media, social media and the internet.

Television – A Brief Reflection
When I was a boy, television was still in its infancy and there was initially only one channel, the BBC, followed a few years later by ITV. Only a few folks in our street had a television and if you were lucky enough that your mate's parents had one, you could sometimes go and watch theirs when something special was on at night. Programmes started

around 9am with some stuff for tots such as *Andy Pandy* and *Watch with Mother*. There were some other programmes until about 2pm then the test card would appear which was just a still picture on the screen for several hours during the day and light music would be playing in the background that mums used to listen to whilst doing the housework. Programmes started again at around 5pm with the BBC news followed by the likes of *Coronation Street* which was the original TV Soap. Programmes ended at 11pm with the 'Epilogue' when some dreary old vicar would drone on for about five minutes about something vaguely religious. Then an announcement would be made from the BBC that the network was closing for the night and that was it. The sound of a click and the screen disappeared into a small dot and programmes for the day had ended. I know that might sound as if it was a hundred years ago or more but it was only during my lifetime, a mere sixty years. In that relatively short period of time, television and other media technology has gone from those humble beginnings to what we have today.

At that time, during my own formative years, and for all the generations that went before, children and young people were predominantly influenced by their parents, their immediate family, their extended family of grannies, granddads and aunts and uncles. Outside of that were the neighbours, the local community and of course, school. Furthermore, cinema was something you only attended occasionally and there were only a handful of film released each year. Films that were subject to strict categories of censorship by the British Board of Film Censors, aimed at ensuring that children and young people were not exposed to inappropriate content.

Parents and grandparents, just consider now for a moment the astounding and quite unbelievable difference between then and now.

Television − A Significant Influence
Of course TV, Video, Film, DVDs etc. have all gradually developed and progressed since then. However, that it was in

fact gradual for many years should be borne in mind. For around thirty years there were only BBC and ITV with Channel 4 not coming into existence until 1982. It is really only since then, particularly in the last twenty years or so that there has been such a huge increase in the volume, diversity and range of available choices of all these forms of viewing media.

Not only is there now twenty-four hour mainstream television on numerous networks and umpteen platforms for 'catch up TV' so you can, and I quote the adverts, 'watch what you want anytime and anywhere', but we can also view box sets of television programmes and series so that the viewer can, and again I quote 'gorge themselves' by viewing entire series all at once. The ever-expanding range of viewing options includes the likes of TV on Demand, STV Player, BBC iPlayer, My5 and Netflix, to name just a few. The list however goes on and on. It really is quite incomprehensible compared to just a generation ago. Furthermore, I'm sure you will have realised some time ago that as far as mainstream television is concerned, the 9pm 'watershed' aimed at safeguarding children and young people from inappropriate television content is now completely redundant.

There is considerable official evidence that regular and habitual 'screen viewing' can be highly habit forming and addictive. That is precisely why TV and film etc. is a constantly burgeoning industry. Adults are addicted to it inasmuch that it is now normal for people to spend several hours and often much more, each and every day in front of a television screen. Society has become addicted to it. Furthermore, society has become increasingly informed, influenced, shaped and significantly conditioned by it. Whether we like to admit it or not television has become a significant part of many people's everyday lives. Furthermore, as all of these viewing options, increasingly wide range of choice and the option to view any of it at any time, unrestricted by previous TV programme times has increased over the years and so have our viewing habits.

Accompanying this developing trend over the past two decades has been the development of the personal computer, the iPad and the smartphone. These devices have had the effect of completely freeing the viewer from the constraints of having to sit in front of a television to being able to watch all of the above and much, much more on the privacy of their own personal 'screen'.

I'm really addressing this book to those who have children or grandchildren in the age range of two to sixteen years of age. Yes, I really do mean two years of age. My reason will become evident.

Smartphones – The New Influence

Now I would like to address the phenomenal advancement of personal hand-held media and communication devices. I am of course referring to smartphones, tablets, iPads and so on. Their fairly recent introduction has been accompanied by a quite remarkable blanket acceptance by society to readily embrace this hitherto unknown and unprecedented technology. A technology that has never existed before in all the millennia of human history. But now, in the space of only two decades has found a place in all of our homes, our jacket pockets and our handbags. To the extent that very many (if not most) people have their 'phone' with them at all times. I emphasise 'phone' because as we know they are so much more than that. Our personal hand-held devices are also our instant access library on every subject on earth and every news platform.

They also serve as our home office, our diary, our media centre, our music store, camera, photo album and much more. We can use them for instant access to other people anywhere in the world at any time. With a couple of taps we are instantly connected to an ever increasing variety of social media platforms such as Facebook, Twitter, Snapchat, Instagram and many more, with new options appearing all the time.

With a tap we can connect instantly to networks such as Google and other platforms to the World Wide Web. Just think about that for a minute – the World Wide Web.

And here is the very point of this book: We are far too readily placing these devices into the hands of our children and young people.

The Social Impact of the Smartphone

Although this technological phenomenon is relatively very new and its long term effects as yet completely unknown, its existence is already in such a short time, changing individual behaviour and society in general. It is now commonplace to encounter people walking towards you in the street wherever you go, eyes glued to their smartphone with little regard to whether they walk into you.

On public transport it is almost impossible not to be afflicted by someone talking loudly on a smartphone about just about anything, with no apparent consideration for others. The same applies to airports, restaurants and other public places. Whilst visiting a large town just outside London recently and deciding to visit the local park on a Sunday morning, I couldn't help notice that almost everyone was walking about like zombies, staring at their devices. Mothers pushing babies in prams and an entire family comprising both parents and three kids aged about seven to fifteen were all silently engrossed in their smartphones as they blindly walked along. A sort of new take on a family walk in the park I suppose!

So often whilst in conversation with someone, their phone will ring and they feel compelled to answer it immediately, or it has to be viewed each time a ping indicates a new message, email or whatever. People are also now commonly phoning or texting whilst driving. What can possibly be so important or pressing that so many people are routinely prepared to risk their lives and the lives of others by being dangerously distracted by what in most cases is trivial which could have been dealt with before or after their journey? In recent years, there have been many reports of serious and fatal road accidents caused by people using their phones whilst driving; including quite unbelievable reports of people texting whilst driving at speeds of eighty miles an hour or more. Furthermore, it is already very noticeable in many domestic and social settings that parents allow and indeed encourage very small children to have a hand-held device as a means of entertaining or occupying themselves. Often, however, it is also an extremely convenient and effective means of simply pacifying them whilst the adults can get on with something else or just to get some peace. But at what cost in the long term? I am sure anyone who has done this will be only too aware of the drama and the tantrums when they try to take the device from the child. It doesn't take a genius to figure out that all this attention to the distracting, pervasive and all-absorbing, instantly available, instantly gratifying and ever-present 'screen' must surely and inevitably be having a dramatic and drastic effect on individual human behaviour, on the very fabric of social interaction and on society as a whole. And the very fabric of society as we all know is the family.

The Dangers of the Smartphone

Information, influences, images and knowledge that up until now parents, grandparents, schools and society in general have historically and traditionally guarded young minds from, is now being streamed to them, undiluted and uncensored from every conceivable source anywhere, anytime and all the time. And they have access to it in the palm of their hand.

And it has access to them.

When we as parents and grandparents thoughtlessly allow our children and young people to have unsupervised and unrestricted use of these media devices, we are in effect handing over our parental influence, guidance and control to total strangers.

Why? Because what they see and hear, starting from a very early age, will shape their thinking, impact their moral values and inform their view of the world, especially because they may be absorbed in their devices for several hours every day.

There are many examples just on mainstream television alone that increasingly seek to project a false image of the 'modern family'.

For example, there a plethora of soaps that almost invariably portray dysfunctional families, dysfunctional marital relationships and an array of 'types' of family structures as the norm.

One recent advert by BT promoting broadband boasts that with super-fast broadband in the home, every member of the family could all be in different parts of the house, each on their own iPad, iPhone, laptop or whatever, happily gaming, streaming, surfing the web etc. Now isn't that a dream worth pursuing?

Quite the contrary, I'm sure you'll agree. It's more like a plot from a futuristic nightmare science-fiction film. It's like something from a future dystopian culture where normal family life is a thing of the past and everyone lives in their own cyber reality, separated, distracted and absorbed by endless media streams and images.

However, the reality is that this is tragically already happening all around us.

The thing about the technology we are dealing with here and the social trends that are accompanying it is that we are placing into the hands of our children the very means by which they can be daily influenced and conditioned – by *other* people. And it begins just as soon as we allow them to access these devices. You might say, what harm can it do to give my two–five-year-old a tablet that only has Disney or similar cartoons loaded onto it? My answer is this: if their use is not strictly controlled and limited, your child will easily become used to it and reliant upon it. Watching Disney etc. will only be the beginning. It will also detract from normal play which is and has always been an essential aspect of healthy development and growth. Furthermore we are inadvertently conditioning our children during their most impressionable and formative years to believe that these devices are an indispensable, integral and essential part of everyday life. No more so than when so many children observe their own parents constant and habitual absorption in their own smartphones and iPads etc.

Social Media Platforms

It is of major concern that our teenagers and younger children are already in the grip of what is already officially recognised as addiction to social media platforms whereby they have become obsessed with having to stay constantly in contact with their friends and peers for fear of feeling left out. Youngsters have always had to cope with bullying at school. Previously it was at least mostly confined to school hours, now, as is widely reported in the media, 'cyber bullying' is already a growing social problem. A young person today, feeling compelled to constantly check-in on social media, can thereby be afflicted by the bullies at any time and all the time.

It seems that everywhere I go, this all-prevailing absorption in the smartphone is staring me in the face. I try to ignore it but I can't. I constantly ask myself, is no one else noticing this? Is no one else concerned about this?

I was in a restaurant in London very recently for an evening meal with friends. A family at the next table were also enjoying an evening out. But both girls aged around thirteen and fifteen years of age each had their device on the table beside their plate. They weren't actually using them but every fifteen minutes or so they briefly checked them. It was as if, they were there with their parents, but they weren't 'really there'. Their attention and interests were clearly elsewhere. I wonder where? Do you suppose their parents knew where? It could quite literally have been anywhere. They could have been communicating with anyone, anywhere, about absolutely anything. These girls were in the company of their parents, however their parents had absolutely no influence or control regarding what was going on in their daughters' lives, even though they were sitting around the same table. But remember, we are not just talking about phone calls or texts to friends, even though texting itself is creating the tragic reality of 'sexting' amongst youngsters. We are also dealing with internet sites. Sites that deal with every subject imaginable, including social media platforms where they can be communicating about absolutely anything; and chat-rooms in which they can be linked to anyone, anywhere from around the world.

This kind of scenario, which is already becoming a cultural norm, serves to clearly represent the inherent dangers of uncensored and uncontrolled access to the internet in all of its forms by our children and young people.

The previous day, I was down by the river for a pub lunch with my family and friends. It was a beautiful summer day. Boats, water, ducks, maritime activity etc., you get the picture. The place was very busy, I tried my very hardest to just enjoy all that the riverside traditionally has to offer – and not to notice – but there it was again. Entire families engrossed in smartphones after eating their meals or even actually during the meal. Next to me a boy of about eight with his parents, was bent over, with his hands shielding his eyes, straining to keep the sun off his 'screen'. His mum and dad privately engrossed in their own smartphones.

Internet Content
There is growing national concern amongst children's agencies and child health professionals about the increasing rate of mental health referrals relating to our young people, statistically linked directly to exposure to internet content, as well as the damaging influences of unregulated and unmonitored interaction on social media platforms. There are many figures from research already available that are raising extreme concerns about the effects of explicit 'adult' material being accessed by children and young people and the very serious emotional, psychological and developmental damage

17

this can cause. The same research reveals that parental control settings can be easily by-passed by young people, who are very often more technically competent than their parents. Of additional and even more concern is how very young children, already accustomed to being able to use hand held devices through watching children's sites on platforms such as YouTube etc., can accidentally access such materials and imagery.

It is not the purpose of this book to catalogue reams of statistics.

One ongoing major government study that should be mentioned here however is outlined below:

"Primary pupils in Scotland are being given 'porn awareness' classes amid fears they are being damaged by graphic images online. Children as young as ten are being warned that downloading sexual images and videos can lead to addiction, mental health problems, abuse and revenge porn.

The lessons have been created in response to fears that children are accessing porn more easily and at an ever-younger age – and that parents are failing to stop them.

Campaigning charity, the Reward Foundation is piloting lessons at two schools in Lanarkshire and Edinburgh – with talks over several more to follow. Lessons discussing harmful aspects of pornography are being given to primary seven pupils and various secondary school year groups.

The classes could soon be rolled out Scotland-wide, with backing from the Scottish government.

Last month, the World Health Organisation included 'compulsive sexual behaviour' as a mental health disorder for the first time.

But the Reward Foundation believes there is too much focus on sexual relationships, when 80 percent of addictions are believed to be related to porn."

Chief Executive Mary Sharpe said: 'Children are being exposed to hard-core internet pornography at an increasingly younger age.

'Many have unfiltered access to the internet through smartphones and tablets. It is this kind of exposure that has been linked to an increase in child-on-child sexual abuse and mental health issues.' She added: 'Parents can use filters on home computers but often forget to, or children find ways around them. Sex education is compulsory in England but not Scotland, where councils and head teachers are given greater freedom over that part of the curriculum. However, even where schools cover sexual education, they ignore pornography,' warned Ms Sharpe.

She said: 'It's the elephant in the room that everyone hopes will go away. It won't and the kids are the ones suffering the most.' The lessons will not involve the kids being shown anything approaching pornographic images, but will focus on the health and legal consequences. They look at how sexual images affect the brain and lead to addiction – and how spreading explicit pictures without consent can lead to prosecution. The pilot is expected to run until the end of September. A Scottish Government spokesman said: 'The dangers of sexually explicit online content are well documented. We would encourage schools to look at ways of helping pupils to avoid harm.'

Eileen Prior, executive director of Connect, a charity representing parents in Scottish education, said: 'There will be many parents who will support the approaches outlined by the Reward Foundation, but equally, there will be parents concerned about the content. The lessons will be led by teachers, but using materials by the Reward Foundation. Porn has been viewed online by 65 percent of 15–16-year-olds, 48 percent of 11–16-year-olds and 28 per cent of 11–12-year-olds, according to a 2016 NSPCC report.' Dr Ether Quayle, lecturer in clinical and health psychology at Edinburgh University, said: 'Very early exposure to pornography can be related to elevated use in later life. We need to face up to any embarrassment we feel about this issue and we must – especially with sexting, appreciate the pressures young people are under to conform.'

Internet Chat Rooms

Internet chat rooms are already causing extreme social concern, with frequent stories in the media of adults connecting with total strangers, taking their word that they are who they say they are only to find, often when it is too late, that they are not.

That children and young people can also freely do this in the privacy of their own bedrooms or elsewhere should send shudders down the spine of every parent, grandparent and society at large.

There have been numerous cases reported in the media where children as young as twelve years of age have innocently connected with sexual predators online, with tragic and sometimes fatal consequences. We surely must ask ourselves this question: just what on earth is a child doing accessing such sites and chat rooms (which are commonplace and easily accessible on the internet) clearly unsupervised? Let me take you back to the BT advert mentioned above, with every member of the family in a separate part of the house, each independently engrossed in their own online or media 'cyber' world.

Is this really the kind of society we want? Is this really our idea of family life? Is this really what we want for our children? Has the world gone mad? Seriously!

The Arrival of the Smartphone

Here is a brief chronology of the evolution of the smartphone. These dates are not precise but are a fairly accurate timeline.

1985 – Personal computers: that is, the old-fashioned bulky television type that sat on the desk in the office or home, were becoming commonplace.

1992 – The Internet was launched.

1996 – The first laptops appeared on the market.

2000 – The first smartphone appeared on the market in the UK.

New Technologies Require Regulation
We see then that the smartphones which the vast majority of us carry around have only been a part of our lives for a mere eighteen years or so. And it is these smartphones that give us unbridled access to all of the technologies already mentioned. Should you be thinking perhaps that I'm just of a certain age, old fashioned, out of touch and on a major downer about new technologies? I can assure you that is absolutely not the case. This technology is truly amazing and dramatically life-changing. It represents so many advantages and has great potential to enhance education, inform and connect friends, families, communities, businesses, commerce and nations. And to shape our world for the better. However, like other previous significant technological developments, it also has the potential to cause great harm.

For example: The splitting of the atom released the capacity to create nuclear fusion, with the potential to create an unlimited affordable source of energy and power for industrial and commercial use.

However, it is also used to create nuclear weapons i.e., weapons of mass destruction on a global scale. Such technology therefore has to be harnessed and regulated. It has to be governed to ensure it supports life and not destroys it.

Another example is the invention of the motor car, which went on to totally impact, enhance and transform our everyday lives and societies across the world. Let's not forget however that its use is subject to a wide range of statutory legislation as well as rules and regulations for every driver. Without these the car would be lethal and destructive and there would be constant carnage on our roads. In fact it just wouldn't be safe to use them.

But we now have the 'super-highway:' a media and communications technological global highway with many millions of people on it, every day and absolutely all the time. Many saying what they want, doing what they want, filming what they want and broadcasting what they want and for whatever reason they want. It is all potentially accessible to absolutely anyone who has a smartphone etc.

However, quite unlike previous technological global phenomenon such as the containment of nuclear power or all of the legislation and rules around owning and using a car, this 'technological media and communications highway' has absolutely no rules, no restrictions and no boundaries. Furthermore, it is completely unregulated by any rules or regulations. Neither is it subject to any standards of decency, morality or any other kind of sanctions whatsoever.

As such, it has hitherto unprecedented potential to cause significant and lasting harm.

Is it an Age Thing?

If you are aged, say around forty years and over, you may well be thinking, I personally don't see a problem, I only use my smartphone for phoning, texting, the news, booking flights and maybe purchasing stuff. It's great, it's handy and it's made life easier. If you are a parent or grandparent you will no doubt also be thinking, but our smartphones are great for keeping in touch with the kids and that's got to be all good, right? Absolutely, that is all good. It's a great example of this new technology being used for good. However this book is not aiming to address particular concerns about you. As an adult your ideas are already formed. You are already mature. You know right from wrong, good from evil, truth from lies and so on.

Furthermore, you and your generation – and all the generations that went before – had all the protection, supervision, guidance and control that your parents, grandparents, local communities, peer groups etc., had to offer. Additionally, by means of these factors you were given time to grow, to mature, to learn discernment. To have information, facts and realities revealed to you incrementally. In other words, you were shielded and protected from certain things until you were able to understand them and deal with them. Now however, with the societal proliferation, cultural acceptance and individual personal ownership of the smartphone and such devices, there exists a very real and present danger that children and young people today will have that all stripped away from them. Why? Because they could potentially be exposed to absolutely anything, beginning quite literally from the time they are able to access and view a screen.

Even as I am writing, STV news is reporting an up to 26% increase over the last few years in depression amongst children of varying ages, resulting in a significant upsurge in the use of anti-depressants and psychological therapies. I wonder why? I personally believe that we are merely seeing the very small tip of what will prove to be a very large 'iceberg'. We should all be very concerned for our children and our grandchildren. And indeed for all children and young people everywhere. For this generation and the ones that follow. The concern for them is this: by means of this media and communications revolution, because that's what it is, a technological − revolution, yes you can reach your children and families anytime and anywhere − *but so can anyone else.* How? Because your children and young people carry the means of contact and communication in their pockets and what they can potentially see and hear is entirely outwith the knowledge, control, influence and supervision of their parents and others closest to them.

Revolution

Revolutions change things, they radically and rapidly turn things around, hence the term revolution, to revolve. And cultural revolutions are predominantly aimed at influencing the younger generations, with the older generation not knowing what it was all about until later.

By which time it's too late. Then they wonder what hit them.

What has become known as the Arab Spring started in Tunisia in 2011 when the populations of a number of North

African and Middle Eastern countries simultaneously rose up in rebellion against their governments.

Their ability to do so was largely attributed to those populations, predominantly the younger generation, having access to social media platforms where the initial propaganda and ease and availability of instant communications spread the message and the coordination of the revolutions like wildfire. That particular revolution is ongoing and is changing those societies forever. Tragically, in doing so it has thrown many of them into social turmoil and chaos. There are however many forms of revolution.

Radicalisation and Recruitment

We are also now only too familiar with news reports about ordinary citizens suddenly committing acts of violence and terror, supposedly in the name of an extremist religious ideology.

A common feature of such incidents is that the people closest to those individuals are as shocked and surprised as anyone else by the seemingly sudden and dramatic change in their behaviour. It transpires in so many of those cases that the individual was radicalised by online propaganda, interconnected with related social networking sites.

This is a new and rapidly increasing social phenomenon, connected directly to the internet and social media:

Individuals can be radically ideologically conditioned without even those closest to them knowing anything about it until it's too late and the damage has already been done. How? Because at some point and for some reason *and because they could*, they entered a world alien to the social and cultural norms that surround them. And they do so within the complete privacy and exclusivity of their personal device. As such, a young person can over a short period of time potentially be dramatically influenced and impacted even whilst drinking juice with friends in a cafe or youth club or sitting at home surrounded by family members.

But exposure to and indoctrination by extremist religious or political ideologies is only one kind of corrosive and destructive influence that seriously endangers our children and young people today.

Sexual Radicalisation

Across democratic societies globally, politically militant movements driven by highly organised special interest groups of ideological activists and pressure groups have a specific agenda aimed at driving radical social, moral and cultural change.

Their aim is to change the meaning of marriage.

Their aim is to change the very concept of the family structure.

Their aim is to change the established norms and parameters of sexuality. To the extent that they want sexual identity and gender terminology such as male/female or girl/boy abolished and ultimately made illegal by having our laws changed.

You will have your own personal views concerning these matters. Whatever they are, these influences are becoming increasingly prevalent throughout society, the effect of which will directly and personally affect your children and grandchildren now and for generations to come should they continue.

Furthermore, a fundamental core objective of these lobbyists and pressure groups is to have compulsory sex education in schools introduced to primary school children on the basis, they claim, it will create, and I quote:

'A more tolerant society by instilling in children (from primary school onwards) non-discriminatory attitudes that celebrate diversity and inclusiveness.'

The school sex education curriculum proposed would encompass the presentation of all forms of sexual and gender identity and practice as socially and morally permissible and acceptable. The most recent media coverage reveals that this should include the primary school children themselves being taught that they can choose their own gender.

You might be asking, so where does our youngsters exposure to the internet and social media platforms come into this? Well, here's just one example from a recent press article.

Teenagers who question their biological gender often have friends who have become transgender, researchers found. Twenty one percent of teenagers and young adults who suddenly questioned their gender identity after puberty had one or more friend who 'came out' as transgender around the same time, according to a study of their parents. US researchers surveyed 254 parents of youngsters aged 11 to 27 with gender dysphoria – the distress of feeling you are a different gender to the one you were born with – that came on after puberty. In 86.5 of cases, the children were reportedly the second, third or fourth within their friendship group to question their gender. Study author, Dr Lisa Littman, from Brown University in Provence, Rhode Island, said: 'Of the parents who provided information about their child's friendship group, about a third responded that more than half of the kids in the friendship group became transgender identified.'

One parent said their child had seen a 'great increase in popularity' by identifying as transgender, adding: 'Being trans is a gold star in the eyes of the other teens.'

One in five parents reported an increase in their child's social media use around the same time as their gender dysphoria, with parents suspecting YouTube 'transition' videos had influenced this. The study says: 'The description of cluster outbreaks of gender dysphoria occurring in pre-existing groups of friends and increased exposure to social media/internet preceding a child's announcement of a transgender identity raises the possibility of social contagion. The study, published in the journal PLOS One, recruited parents from websites for those critical of the 'transgendering' of young people. But 88 percent believed transgender people deserved the same rights as everyone else.

I trust that parents and grandparents reading this will already be sufficiently aware and informed on this subject as it is not the purpose of this book to go into great detail on specifics.

The point I am making is this: all of these agendas already permeate society at every level. The militant activists and lobbyist groups driving these changes frequently and intentionally make headlines by challenging established norms and claiming all forms of discrimination against anyone and everyone who disagrees with them. They are seeking to continually and strategically challenge and change moral and societal norms and standards that have existed for millennia.

Norms and standards that placed the family at the very heart of society. And which ensured that children and young people were nurtured and protected by their parents, their grandparents, the wider family unit, schools, governments and society in general.

The 'Message' in the Media

The past twenty years or so in particular has also seen a significant and dramatic shift in what used to be considered by society as morally and socially acceptable on mainstream television and film.

Furthermore this shift in what is now deemed to be acceptable is played out repeatedly every day on our television screens in films and DVD, on internet platforms and across the whole spectrum of social media.

These changing societal attitudes regarding moral behavioural and sexual standards are now openly represented and constantly repeated within the storylines, themes, behaviours and language of all of these forms of media.

All visual media such as films, television, CD, internet etc., carries a 'message'. Whether that message is clear or vague, actual or implied, subliminal or apparent, there is always a message. All such 'messages' use subtle forms of suggestion in order to influence and all such suggestion is reinforced by repetition, continual and constant repetition.

And exposure to repeated visual messages and other media communication, leads in time to individual and societal 'conditioning'. By conditioning I mean that if you see and hear something 'repeated' often enough and from a variety of sources, but without really giving it much thought, you will gradually accept it.

Therein is the unprecedented power today (to constantly repeat and reinforce the 'message') of the personal hand-held, instantly accessible 'screen'.

The screen on your children and young person's smartphone or tablet.

The smartphone or tablet they can view anything, anywhere and at any time − over and over again (suggestion-influence-repetition).

The smartphone or other such device therefore has the capacity and the potential unprecedented and unparalleled in all of human history − to thereby condition our children and young people. And to do so quickly.

To condition them in so many ways, some of which I have already alluded to.

To condition them without you even knowing about it.

The '60s' Revolution

There was a cultural revolution during the '60s' when I was a teenager. It saw the advent of rock-music, heralded in by pop-music and pop culture. It was the era of the Beatles and the Rolling Stones and scores of other bands and music acts from across the USA and Britain. It was the era of 'free love', 'psychedelia' and 'sex, drugs and rock and roll'. It was the birth of million seller singles and albums, the music charts − and the beginning of massive tours by bands who sold-out stadiums (and made millions of dollars) across America and far beyond. Records and tours that 'sold' the music − and its 'message' to my generation. Simply by constant and continual 'suggestion and repetition'.

That revolution profoundly impacted and shaped western society and culture. And it continues to do so to this day. Its many negative effects are now seen every day across society in many forms, such as:

1. The common and widespread use of drugs with all the associated personal, family, social and societal problems and misery associated with it. And it's well-documented impact upon crime and violence throughout society.

2. The profound liberalisation of attitudes regarding sexual conduct and sexual responsibility, with all the associated consequences of unwanted teen pregnancies and children born outside the care, support and security of the traditional family unit. And the associated negative and destructive impact upon society.

3. An overall societal swing towards what can most succinctly be described as individualism and hedonism. Individualism in that – it's all about me, my rights, my choices, my pleasure, my wants and desires. Hedonism in that life is about having fun, and if I want to get drunk, take drugs, have indiscriminate sex with anyone and everyone I want, then that's up to me, that's my business. And that the consequences for me or anyone else are irrelevant.

But you need to understand: that WAS the message of the '60s' revolution 'Sex, drugs and rock and roll'. That message was well summed up in the lyrics of one '60s' classic track: 'If it feels good – do it!'

It was the prevailing message contained within the music, music that was purchased in its millions and listened to over and over and over again by an entire generation of young people.

That was the tune that was played – and society danced to it. And we are still dancing to it today. Styles and genres of music have come and gone from then until now but the core message remains the same. And that message has evolved. It is increasing liberal, increasing sexually permissive and increasingly hedonistic. But this book is neither an analysis nor in-depth commentary of these things. I mention the '60s' revolution as a means of comparison to what I want to say next. And it's this:

During the '60s the age range of young people initially impacted by the beginning of the huge ideological and cultural change, carried and driven by the new style of music and those who played it, was around thirteen years of age upward. Like children that age today, they lived at home with their parents. But unlike children today, they didn't have tablets or smartphones.

They were exposed to the 'pop' revolution initially through television. Television that their parents and grandparents also watched. Furthermore, it was the norm then for families to watch television together. As such, their parents and other adults in their lives were also watching what was going on. So they at least knew what their kids were listening to and watching even if they didn't approve. There was therefore still a strong degree of censure, control, protection and parental influence. Today however that is increasingly no longer the case. It is now a long time since the '60s and society has been gradually and constantly changing since then and now accepts, whether consciously or not, different standards of morality and conduct. Gradual changes of morality and conduct that we have all been exposed to and conditioned by. When I say 'conditioned by', I mean that whilst many people do not agree with many aspects of these changes and do not in fact personally adopt or embrace them, society as a whole has been conditioned. This conditioning is clearly reflected today in our society's lifestyles, behaviours and personal and social habits. And in our legislations and laws that are being gradually repealed, amended and replaced by new laws.

A Major Difference

Previous generations, mine included, have been generally, what I would call 'gradually acclimatised' to change. That is, we were exposed to certain facts and realities about life in a way that was age appropriate. As such, we were allowed to become sufficiently mature and emotionally and psychologically developed before we had to face or deal with certain things. To put it another way, we were protected until we were ready. That protection came from the presence and the influence of our parents, from the extended family, from school and from society at large. A society that held to certain moral and ethical standards. Moral and ethical standards that were enshrined in laws and legislations and which had been for hundreds of years. Laws and legislation that upheld and valued the family, civic and individual responsibility and accountability and the protection of children and young people.

Alarmingly − this is increasingly no longer the case.

In the '60s, my generation underwent radical change. But we were buffered by our parents and by longstanding, firmly established moral standards and societal norms. Yes, change came but we grew with it and we had time to grow with it. We were able to make up our own minds what was right or what was wrong. To accept or reject the new culture, which was predominantly carried on the winds of music and lyrics. If a young person then wanted to avoid the disapproval of their parents regarding what they were listening to and the influence it was having on them, they could escape into their room and play their records whilst surrounded by posters of their favourite bands or pop 'idols'. But they were already older and society with its protective influences and social norms and boundaries was still all around them.

But today, it's very different. Society is changing so much that the very concept of normal is threatened. Threatened by the special interest groups, the political activists, lobbyists and pressure groups who are forcing an ideology and a world-view that was 'seeded' in the social, cultural and sexual revolution of the '60s. It was seeded then and has been growing since. It is however no longer just social, cultural and ideological, it is also strongly political. From a social, cultural and ideological perspective it has already permeated the news media and the film, music and entertainment industries.

From a political perspective, it has so far succeeded in having many of our laws repealed or amended and new ones put in their place. It will seek to continue to do so, if allowed to, until it achieves its objectives.

My point is this: the societal norms that set a benchmark and boundaries which previously and historically acted as role models and buffer zones, are increasingly no longer there. The result is that children and young people today, unlike previous generations, have much less of an established frame of reference. Faced with something wrong, dangerous, fake, false, manipulative or immoral, they increasingly have little to compare it with.

Can You Believe It?

This takes me to another related issue and that issue is the mainstream news media and the very many other news and information platforms that exist online. We have increasingly moved into the realm of 'sound bites' instead of actual news reporting. Mainstream TV networks merely provide snippets of local international and world news and it is now recognised that most networks are strongly biased both politically and ideologically. As such they essentially only report what they want and how much on any subject they want, depending on their bias. Of course they wouldn't admit that. The truth is however that 'Investigative Journalism' has very little place in mainstream news media anymore. 'News' these days is little more that the news channel repeating what the opinion of their biased sources and sponsors tell them. There is little or no investigation involved. Investigation by its very description indicates an investigation into a matter. That is, taking into account the views and realities of all sides of an issue and then reporting that in a factual and unbiased fashion.

The natural conclusion to this is that if people rely on such biased sound bites they will come to believe them rather that learning the facts of a matter for themselves. The recent phenomenon of 'fake news' has served to confirm this. We have thereby made a massive leap from, is it accurate or inaccurate to, is it actually true or false?

Add to that the fact that many people increasingly look online for news items. This can of course have advantages by providing the reader with a range of diverse versions of events or sides to a story. However, it is more likely that many people will search for information that reinforces their personal views and opinions rather than read alternative views that will expose or challenge their own. Thereby the biased 'sound bites' already absorbed are merely reinforced.

Due to the internet, society is being swamped, overloaded and bombarded with information which includes information and news about everything and from everywhere. Subsequently, many people merely scan news items online whilst invariably being distracted by the deluge of adverts and wholly unrelated visual media clips that very often accompany the actual news item.

My view is that all of this, rather than consolidate communities and society in general around common and mutually beneficial issues and themes, it scatters and fragments the sense of national cohesion.

New Technologies – A Better Society?

The internet and social media platforms have opened society up to a 'cyber world' of seemingly endless (and often pointless) communication, information and issues.

Using internet sites, the likes of YouTube and the wide array of social media platforms such as Facebook in addition to chat rooms, blogs etc., so many people seem to find the time to spew out their views and opinions, seemingly about anything, everything and anyone.

The most vile and hurtful things are said to and about other people. This is now a very common problem across the wide range of social media platforms and one which is now routinely affecting every day communication. Politicians, national figures, media personalities and celebrities are also maligned, insulted and threatened. The term 'troll' has taken on an entirely different meaning. No one is safe from this and the law seems powerless to stop it. It can be likened to living in a constant state of road rage. We may all at one time or another raged abuse at a driver in another vehicle. It's momentary, reactive and plainly wrong to behave this way. And we all know it. It passes and we feel bad. The fact is we wouldn't dream of behaving in such a way if we were face to face with that person. We behave that way because we can. Because there are no consequences (we hope). There is distance (and a vehicle) between us. We are generally moving at the time and we will never see them again. In the street we would be civil and courteous to that person and probably even apologise to them if *they* accidentally bumped into us.

What I mean is, the 'distance' made available 'behind the keyboard' is not unlike the distance between us and the other driver when we are behind the wheel. But whilst road rage is for most people a rare occurrence, social media platform 'rage' is becoming a cultural norm. It is comment without concern, communication without consequence and dialogue without either discretion or discernment. It is faceless and often anonymous aggression and hostility. I believe these factors combined are contributing to a society which is becoming increasingly intolerant of the opinions of others and which is resistant to rational, civil, well-informed, measured discussion and debate.

Furthermore, due to being daily immersed in a deluge of information, opinion and e-media distractions, much of it trivial, many people are not in touch with or as informed as they used to be about the things that really matter and the issues that actually and directly affect their everyday lives.

They are however exposed to the perpetual and constant barrage of biased news and information sound bites that many are addicted to viewing online and following on social media. As well as the time spent on a whole array of social media platforms, chat rooms, films, videos and online games etc.

Statistics vary but it is currently estimated that many teenagers and adults up to around thirty years of age spend an average of five hours every day on their smartphones. It is reasonable to assume that younger children will do likewise in due course. To put it another way: society is rapidly becoming shaped and conditioned by the influence and the propaganda of the mass media/culture machine. And with the advent and mass proliferation of the personal hand-held device, that is now more achievable on a mass scale and across all ages, including small children and young people, than ever before.

Therefore, by allowing our children and young people to have unsupervised, unmonitored and unregulated personal access to hand held devices, we are also potentially putting them in the way of corrosive, negative and damaging influences.

The New Revolution

The 'message' of the revolution of the '60s was carried on the winds of music; music that everyone knew was out there and that was bought in the form of singles and LPs. Therefore, the means of the message had to be purchased and brought into the family home, into the young persons' life or watched on TV or at concerts.

It dramatically impacted teenagers, youngsters of a certain level of maturity, who were physically, emotionally and psychologically already transitioning from childhood into adulthood. But that was then and this is now.

The 'message' today is carried not just on the winds of music, which of course remains a highly potent and influential force, but is carried on the wings of Internet Technology and Social Media in all of its forms and formats. It no longer has to be bought, like records or CDs from shops, viewed on TV or heard at concerts. It is all now instantly available and accessible on a touch screen, without anyone having to go anywhere or buy anything. Every minute of every hour, twenty-four hours a day, seven days a week, three hundred and sixty-five days a year, non-stop.

But more crucially and alarmingly, unlike any societal/cultural revolutions that have gone before, this one is very different. Why? Because it has free and open access, not just to teenagers but also to young children – our children. From the moment they are given a tablet or smartphone they are susceptible to the addictive element of viewing, the addictive element of so-called entertainment and the conditioning influences of the unprecedented changes that are taking place all around us today. So many and such frighteningly radical and far reaching changes, that many adults are barely able to absorb, keep up with or understand.

Yet we are in extreme danger of exposing our children and our young people to these realities long before they are able to cope with them, let alone understand them.

Teamwork

You will have noticed throughout this book that when I refer to parents, I also always refer to grandparents. That is very intentional and here is why:

After parents, grandparents are the most closely involved with their children.

My intention in writing this book is to raise an alarm about the dangers I have already outlined and in the hope that both parents and grandparents will read it because parents and grandparents quite literally need to be 'reading from the same page' on this issue.

They need to agree on how to regulate, control and limit the time their children/grandchildren spend using smartphones etc.

They need to be in agreement regarding the terms that their children/grandchildren are to be allowed to use smartphones etc.

They need to ensure that their children/grandchildren are properly informed and educated regarding the do's and don't's of using these devices.

They themselves also need to set examples of appropriate use by using smartphones etc., sparingly in front of their children/grandchildren and excluding or restricting their use during mealtimes etc.

Also, as it is commonplace to ask our children what they did or learned at school that day, we should also be routinely asking them – what did you watch or learn on your smartphone or tablet today?

Very serious consideration should also be given to what is an appropriate age to give a child a smartphone in the first place, if indeed at all. A simple cell phone for ease of contact should be all a younger person needs. Also, there are many other non-internet devices that can be used for games and educational resources.

Another reason I specifically include grandparents is that, as stated earlier, the smartphone has only been around a mere eighteen years. Grandparents are therefore much more aware than their own grown up kids that these devices are actually not indispensable. They still have an important parenting role therefore when it comes to reminding their grandchildren's parents to use these devices appropriately and responsibly.

Who Sets The Rules?

One of the examples I used earlier concerning this technological superhighway is that of motor vehicles on the road. The actual traffic highway which is governed and controlled by many laws, rules and regulations. Those wanting to 'go onto it' firstly have to be of a certain age. Then they have to be trained by a qualified instructor. They then have to pass a strict and comprehensive driving test. Then and only then are they considered to be competent and safe enough to be granted a licence to go onto the highway. Otherwise they could seriously harm themselves or others.

Not so however with the technological highway of the Internet. There are no laws, no rules, no regulations, no effective safeguards and absolutely no lower age restrictions. It is wide open and free to all. And it's a free-for-all. But at what cost in terms of the emotional, psychological and moral danger and harm to our children and young people? Let me also put it this way, if there was no highway code, no requirements for anyone to have a driver's licence, so that car owners could simply do as they pleased on our roads, would we allow our teenagers to take a car into that chaos? Of course we wouldn't. It would be a recipe for disaster and quite literally and accident waiting to happen.

Consider this: If you don't educate your children/grandchildren about the negative aspects and dangers of the Internet and social media – be absolutely sure of this – no one else will.

If you don't establish parameters and regulations about their use – no one else will.

All the evidence so far clearly points to the fact that these dangers are not something we can hope that politicians, the government or our education system can or will protect our children and young people from.

In today's world, the only truly reliable safeguards our children and young people have is us, their parents and their grandparents. If we do not protect the minds of our children, absolutely no one else will. And if we fail to inform and shape their young minds, someone else most certainly will. More so nowadays than ever before.

Finally, there is considerable social and peer pressure on youngsters to own and use (or wrongly use) a smartphone. However, I believe that parents and grandparents have to stand firm on this particular issue because of its very serious and far-reaching implications. Perhaps though, this is not a bad thing. Rather, perhaps this is an opportunity. An opportunity to reaffirm and re-establish who should in fact be the main influence, guidance and moral compass for our children and young people. Not an ever-shifting society which is in itself desperately in need of direction and not governments or educational institutions.

No, none of these. They are *our* children. They are *our* young people. They are *our* families. It is therefore parents, grandparents and the wider family unit who urgently and immediately need to take control and in many cases – take back control – if we are to effectively safeguard and protect our children and young people both now and into the future.

The Frog and the Boiling Pot

There is an old traditional fable that goes something like this:

A frog was placed in a pot of cold water on a cooker. The frog swam comfortably for quite some time. Then the water was heated a little but the frog didn't notice and continued swimming. After some time the heat was increasing some more. Still the frog failed to notice because it had unconsciously adjusted to the gradually changing temperature of its environment. When the temperature of the water continued to rise, the frog finally began to feel the heat. Sensing imminent danger the frog attempted to jump out of the pot. However, it had been weakened by the effects of its changing environment.

A lesson that can be learned from this fable is that there can be very serious consequences in allowing ourselves to be conditioned by our 'environment' whilst being unaware of the imminent dangers.

Chapter 2
A 21st Century Myth

Have you bought into the 21st century myth? There are many such myths but I want to address just one of them here within the context of this book. The word 'myth' is given numerous dictionary definitions. Here are some of them:

1. An imaginary thing, person or concept.
2. Any invented idea, story or concept.
3. An unproved or false collective belief which is used to justify a social institution.

I want to focus on definition three: An unproved or false collective belief which is used to justify a social institution. There exists within western society a prevalent 'myth' that:

The days in which we live are so fast paced.
There just isn't enough time to do everything.
Life these days is so pressured.
There are so many competing demands.
Things are moving so fast.

And because of this:

Relationships are under pressure.
Families are under pressure.
Family life is under pressure.
Everyone is under pressure.
Modern life is so stressful
Everyone is stressed

But where does all this come from?

Compared to previous generations, as a society we are far wealthier, we have better health, better education, better lifestyles, a more stable society, an absence for over seventy years of domestic military conflict, far more choices and much more leisure time. Surely, logic alone would dictate that such hugely significant and comprehensive individual and collective improvements should lead to a happier, more balanced, more creative and more harmonious life. A life that offers more time − not less, less pressure − not more, less stress − not increased stress, a slower pace − not a faster one. Think about it. It just doesn't make any sense at all. This entire concept of all this 'freneticism' is in fact a myth. It's a complete myth sold to us by the media, by television companies, by filmmakers, by advertisers and others wanting to sell us their products, including by seemingly limitless and ever-newly emerging publication titles of celebrity and lifestyle magazines. 'Lifestyle' magazines − how ironic!

So, we are told we need fast food, faster cars, fast news, faster information, faster trains, faster flights, faster broadband, faster shopping, faster (speed) dating. Fast, fast, fast and ever faster. But for what? So we will all have more time. More time for what? More time to watch television?

More time to watch television programmes. Disconnected, unrelated and largely irrelevant television programmes. More time to watch 'soaps'. Endless, entirely fictitious storylines portraying entirely fictitious characters, written, created and produced by total strangers on behalf of massive media companies for the sole purpose of encouraging people to addictively watch an endless stream of pointless programmes which masquerade under the guise of 'entertainment'.

More time to stare at an ever-increasing range of 'reality shows'. Reality shows which are in 'reality' entirely 'stage-managed' by production companies; shows which almost invariably depict individuals or social groups who enjoy a far higher and more privileged lifestyle than most of the viewers.

An entire society of viewers who are rushing through life. A life that is apparently so pressured and so fast paced and that has so many competing demands but one that very oddly can find the time to stare at a TV screen for an average of five hours every day. Out of a twenty-four hour day period, eight is spent sleeping, another eight on an average working, which leaves eight hours for leisure, recreation and family time. However, for many people across society, an average of five of those eight hours is spent watching television. That amounts to a staggering 62.5% on average of an individual's leisure time. And that only relates to television.

More time to watch Netflix etc. More time to 'catch-up' with catch-up TV, box sets, SKY 'bundles' etc. But why? Why are we willing to rush through life in order to 'save time', so that we can spend that precious time watching other people – other people quite literally, 'acting out' their lives or the fictitious lives of others. Almost entirely fictitious and manufactured lives. It simply doesn't make any sense.

As a society we are in effect 'watching' other people's lives and not even real ones at that, at the expense of living our own.

Hence the total myth of the fast paced, pressured, competing demands of 21st century life. There is, in fact, no more pressure on our time than at any other time throughout modern history. We actually have significantly more time on our hands and far less pressure. But what we are doing is wasting time and we are doing so on a monumental scale.

Just imagine for a moment if you didn't have a television or an iPad or a laptop or a smartphone. Setting aside for a moment the many obvious and positive actual benefits of these things, just think about how much more personal time we would have without them. More time to spend engaging with our families, our spouses, our children. More time talking, more time listening, more time thinking, more time creating, more time reading, more time helping, more time learning, and more time pursuing individual interests instead of being daily and habitually 'interested' in what film, television and all the other mass media companies are pumping out to the 'masses' every minute of every hour of every single day.

Our lives aren't in fact any busier than before. They are no more pressured than before. There is no less time than we had before. There are no more competing demands than previous generations had. No – not if you remove the ever pervasive and terminally invasive and ever increasing flickering screens that seek to demand your attention, your interest – and your time.

Therein is the 21st century myth. The facts are and the actual truth is, that society has been and is being, sold that myth. Sold and peddled by those who benefit from it.

Think about it this way – television... is actually – tele-ported 'vision'. Teleported or telecommunicated into your home, into your life, via your TV, your laptop and more recently your smartphone. Anywhere, anytime, everywhere and all the time.

Tele-Vision. But it's someone else's 'vision', someone else's vision of life, someone else's vision of morality, someone else's vision of right and wrong, someone else's vision of good and bad, someone else's vision of *their* values, someone else's vision of family, someone else's vision of society, someone else's vision of the meaning of life and its purpose, someone else's vision of why we exist and why we are here, someone else's vision – for *your* life, for your family's lives and someone else's vision for *your* children's lives. And we, as individuals and as a society are daily absorbing that vision for more hours a week than full-time students studying at school or university and over a considerably longer period than four or five years.

So what's the solution? That's if you're interested in a solution? The solution is very simple. Switch it off! Take control. Reclaim your time. Reclaim your life. Reclaim your own thoughts. Reclaim your own interests. Reclaim your own opinions. Reclaim your own views. Reclaim what you truly consider to be good and beneficial entertainment for you and your family rather than just keep accepting what is being dished up by the global mega-media factory.

Passively 'consuming' what is being dished up can be compared to living on fast food simply because it is immediately available, immediately 'consumable' and requires absolutely no effort or thought to prepare. But we all now know that fast food or junk food is very bad for your physical health in the long term. However, a balanced diet with the right ingredients produces and maintains good health. Sixty years plus of television and all the other forms of viewing media that has developed over that time is now producing a great deal of junk material which is resulting in poor psychological, emotional, mental, moral and social health.

It's time to take stock. It's time to become educated about this both individually and as a society. It's time to adjust our diet. It's time to really become more 'health' conscious. It's time for us to be 'exercised' in our discernment. It's time to watch what we watch.

Chapter 3
Montag – A Secular Prophecy

Fahrenheit 451, written by Ray Bradbury, was first published in 1953, at a time when, as I mentioned at the start of this book, television was still in its infancy. There were only two channels, a limited selection of programmes, everything was in black and white and all broadcasting stopped at 11 pm. As such, it could hardly be said that television had much of an influence. Yet, as a writer Bradbury astonishingly 'saw' fifty years into the future with amazing accuracy, just what 'television' would become and its influence on human behaviour and society in general. If you've never read the book, I would highly recommend it. In addition to 'seeing' or predicting what television was to become, Bradbury also demonstrated remarkable, almost prophetic, foresight regarding other aspects of 21st century society which are also represented in his book.

Fahrenheit 451 depicts a dystopian future where knowledge and learning is discouraged by the state and the ownership of books is against the law. The central character is a man by the name of Montag. He is employed by the government as a 'Fireman'. However, not a fireman in the sense that we understand. Montag and his colleagues' job was to hunt down anyone who secretly owned books and destroy the books by burning them.

Montag had been married to his wife Mildred for ten years. However, whilst Montag was becoming increasingly concerned about the society he was living in and what it had become, his wife Mildred was totally oblivious to it. The reasons for her obliviousness become very evident. Montag and Mildred clearly had very differing views of life and those differences are powerfully and dramatically depicted in the part of the book that explores their relationship. It's that part of *Fahrenheit 451* that I'm going to very briefly refer to now.

Montag arrived home one night after a particularly harrowing and distressing day doing his job as a fireman. He had also inexplicably kept a book from the house he had set fire to that day. He didn't understand why he took the book, only that he felt compelled to do so. This was a highly irregular thing for a fireman to do. After all, they especially were supposed to uphold the view of the state that all knowledge, other than that sanctioned by the state, was undesirable – and illegal.

Hence, when he arrived home that evening, he was feeling confused and ill at ease. The events of the day and his taking the book were, however, all part of his growing awareness that something was wrong. That something was wrong with his life. Something was wrong with his relationships and something was wrong with the society and culture in which he lived.

When Montag arrived home, his wife Mildred was already in bed. They had separate beds. What follows is a very poignant description of a relationship which was very cold, distant and lacking in intimacy. We discover as the story unfolds why this was the case. Montag attempts to talk to his wife but it's clear that she isn't really listening. She makes trivial small talk but is distracted.

Distracted by the fact that she has a tiny wireless device in her ear pumping out music. The device is described in the book as an audio seashell broadcasting station and that Mildred was listening to it whilst staring at the ceiling.

At the time of the publication of *Fahrenheit 451,* the MP3 player had not even been invented. It was then some years before personal headphones became commonplace and many more before earpieces became the norm. Yet Bradbury describes Mildred as having such a device pressed into her ear. The emphasis in the story is that she used this device a lot. In fact she was constantly either watching the 'screens' in the living room or listening to the music being 'streamed' through her earpiece.

Montag had thought to himself that perhaps he should get one of those audio-seashell broadcasting stations because it was probably the only way he was going to be able to talk to his wife. But then he asked himself what he would actually say. He had then suddenly realised that he really hardly knew her at all.

He tried talking to Mildred again by asking her if she could remember where and when they had first met but she couldn't remember. She had then gone to the bathroom and he could hear the tap water running and the sound of her swallowing. He tried to count how many times she swallowed and how many pills she had taken. He wanted to call out and ask her how many she had taken that night and how many she would take later and not know she had taken them.

Montag then reflected on the fact that there was a 'wall' between him and Mildred. In fact not just one wall but three. 'Walls' that spoke. Walls that contained people. 'Aunts, uncles, cousins and nieces – that lived in those walls.' Talking walls that always seemed to be on, with all those people constantly talking but actually saying nothing. And that Mildred spent her days watching and listening to the walls, so much so that she had come to regard the characters in the many and constant programmes as friends and relatives – actual family. It had started when they were first married with one 'wall' in the living room. Montag had come to see the tragic irony of that because due to her constant daily absorption with those screens, Mildred was in fact enjoying increasingly less real living. Including living out any real relationship with him. One screen had not proved to be enough, soon Mildred wanted a second then a third and they were saving for a fourth. Such were Mildred's priorities. Even when she had friends around for a social evening, it was to follow the latest programme offerings on the screens.

In Fahrenheit 451, Ray Bradbury actually describes these screens as being the entire wall, that having more than one wall as a screen was desirable and having all four walls as screens was Mildred's ultimate objective. He also describes a degree of personal one-to-one live interaction between the viewer and the characters on the screen made possible by technology.

What Bradbury was actually foreseeing all those years ago, as he somehow, no one can possibly know how, looked far and deep into the future and saw huge television screens, even wall screens or wall-mounted television screens as we know them today. Such overbearing screens in every home. In every family home across the country and in every home throughout society. But it's now so much more than just screens on walls. It's screens on laptops, on tablets, on iPads and on devices that we carry with us wherever we go.

Screens that are always on, always present, always audible and always broadcasting. But broadcasting exactly what? And why? And why, we should now perhaps seriously ask ourselves, has society at large allowed television and the internet and social media etc. invade our privacy, invade our personal space and permeate, saturate and dominate so much of our attention, our interest and our time?

There are of course some great programmes on mainstream TV and the associated TV platforms, as well as some great films and a lot of very useful, informative, entertaining and educational content on the internet. However, there is also an awful lot of rubbish and junk and some if it is extremely violent. And much of it is also highly morally and ideologically questionable and therefore potentially very dangerous. In other words, it is again an example of how technology, in this case mass media technology, can be used for good but also used for evil. It can be used to help the individual but also to harm the individual. It can be used to build communities but it can, over time, also destroy them. It can be used to unlimited advantage in the fields of entertainment, education and enlightenment but it is also a highly potent means of mass propaganda and ideological and political manipulation.

I believe that Bradbury was seeing ahead of his own time and what he saw were the dangers for society in the future if it failed to exercise sufficient discernment and control regarding what it allowed to be broadcast and what they allowed themselves to watch, accept and absorb. He also highlights his concerns about the social, moral and political consequences. He clearly anticipated what I have described in the previous paragraph and was portraying the outcome where such mass media accompanied by passive societal acceptance had inevitably resulted in a dystopian rather than a utopian future.

I also believe that we have to quite an alarming extent already journeyed quite a distance down that road as we have increasingly allowed ourselves to be lulled into a sense of passively and largely unquestioningly accepting almost anything that comes onto our screens. The thing is, the 'bad' content is sometimes mixed in with the good content. More worryingly, the 'bad' content is increasingly being 'woven' into what 'used to be' the good content and we are failing to notice the difference. Remember the fable of the frog and the boiling pot!

In chapter one of this book, we considered the early years of television and the '60s' music revolution. We also touched on the beginnings in the '60s of societal recreational drug use. What was light TV entertainment then and the exuberance of a new form of youth music then, are firmly entrenched societal and cultural norms now. What had relatively minor influence initially then has colossal and hugely significant and entrenched influence now. What represented only a small part of our lives then, is in danger of flooding and overwhelming our lives now.

In Bradbury's Montag, we see a man who is still aware that much is wrong with society and that it deeply troubles him. In his wife Mildred, however, we see someone who is quite oblivious to anything and everything. Oblivious because she exists on a diet of 'wraparound' TV. When it's not TV, it's streamed music plugged into her ear. And to carry her through that mindless, careless and pointless existence she is reliant on prescription medication. Medication which is out of control to the extent that she no longer knows how much of it she takes in a day. She is lost to the 'system'. She is a victim of the system. She can therefore be easily controlled by the system. She is no threat to the system, because she doesn't think or feel. In fact she only really thinks or feels in accordance with the 'diet' she is served. What a sad and tragic consequence of how careless and thoughtless exposure to external influences, instilled and perpetuated by unproductive and meaningless mass media in its various forms can have on personal relationships, on families and ultimately on society as a whole.

It is often said that 'you are what you eat'. And it is fairly true to also say that what we eat will shape our bodies. I earnestly believe that from a psychological and emotional perspective that we are also 'what we watch' because what we watch and listen to will shape our minds. And it follows that the 'shape' of our minds will determine our values, our morals and our conduct. Bradbury clearly understood that. He also understood and predicted that television and the technology and technologies that would evolve from it would have unprecedented potential to shape the minds of whole societies – and entire generations.

Fahrenheit 451 depicts a totalitarian society. One where 'thought control' is a reality. The state was in control. Thought, language and literature were all controlled – and enforced by the state.

The masses were 'told' what to think, told what to believe and told what language and terminology they could and could not use. Sounds far-fetched? Think about the subtle yet blatant societal, cultural and political objectives of so-called 'Political Correctness' ideology – and everything that is flowing out from it – and perhaps it's not so far-fetched after all.

Upon reading Bradbury's tragic account of Mildred's obsession with the programmes she constantly watched, if ever there was an accurate description representing the utter banality shot through the storylines of the plethora of so-called 'Soaps' on television in this generation in, *Fahrenheit 451,* Bradbury hits it right on the mark. Did you know that most of today's 'Soaps' have no actual long-term 'storyline?' The writers make it all up as they go along. There are actually no real threads to the scripts. Furthermore, most of the themes within the storylines have multiple optional endings and they are determined by viewer ratings. Yet so many people follow them almost religiously. Almost perhaps, like Mildred, as if they were their actual family. Time spent with 'virtual' imaginary, fictional families instead, like Mildred, of real time spent with their real families. Am I guilty of exaggeration? Is it too far-fetched? You decide!

Reading Bradbury on this subject is a real, or perhaps, surreal case of *Back to the Future.* He foresaw it then. We are living in it now. But what are we going to do about it? Now – leaping forward to the 21st century – dear reader – do we *really* need a TV (or some other screen) in *every* room in the house? Do we really want 'surround sound and visuals' piped into our lives twenty-four hours a day? Do we want to end up like Mildred? And is that really what we want for our children, our grandchildren and for the generations to come?

Chapter 4
Daniel – A Sacred Prophecy

There is a particular story in the Bible which I think is remarkably relevant for today. Even though it is ancient it seems to resonate with the times in which we live as it portrays a very clear and detailed example of the effects of the cultural and ideological proliferation of a society by means of multi mass media indoctrination and conditioning. Like *Fahrenheit 451* this story is also allegorical and symbolic in nature and carries a clear message – and a clear warning.

The story centres around four young friends, who were probably in their teens. They were taken as captives from their home in Israel by the armies of King Nebuchadnezzar the king of Babylon, famous in history for its fabled hanging gardens, around the 6th century BC. Today the remains of the ancient city of Babylon are situated near Baghdad in Iraq. The four young friends were called Shadrach, Meshach, Abednego and Daniel. Because they came from royal lineage in Israel they were to be earmarked for service in the courts of King Nebuchadnezzar. However, they first had to be assimilated into Babylonian culture and were therefore to be subject to a three-year systematic 'programme' of indoctrination. The pun here is irresistible.

They were to be educated in the culture of the Babylonians, taught their language, have their names changed from their native Hebrew names to Persian names and very significantly, placed on a 'daily diet' which was the same diet that King Nebuchadnezzar himself ate.

Whilst all of the elements of the indoctrination process were significant, the 'daily diet' was particularly relevant.

Because, symbolically speaking, therein is the subtle, continuous and continual 'drip' effect of being 'fed' a 'diet' particularly chosen and dictated by someone else. Metaphorically, I am referring here to the media diet which has so profoundly permeated today's society. It is in fact a diet that is chosen and dictated by other people. And we *choose* to 'eat' it. Society has quite literally become obsessive consumers of that product. The planned outcome of the indoctrination period of these four young friends is that they, having been successfully indoctrinated, would take their place in King Nebuchadnezzar's service. In so doing, they will have been conditioned to fit in with their new society and culture. But in the process they will have been permanently separated from their own families, their own people, forgotten their own native culture and even had their true identities completely altered. To put it another way, they will have lost their identity, their individuality and their uniqueness. They will have morphed into the crowd. Become just like everyone else. Without knowing it, they will have, in effect, lost *themselves*.

I genuinely don't think I'm exaggerating when I say I believe this is precisely the effect that today's literal bombardment of an all pervasive mass media culture in all of its forms is having upon society at large and on our young people in particular. The fact is that we are already living daily within a mass media, mass entertainment culture. By 'mass' I mean, everyone is unwittingly being fed the same diet. Society at large is therefore hearing the same message and viewing the same images. Whilst there may be a vast range of programmes, DVDs, internet channels, sites, platforms and so on, the overall and prevailing 'messages' are the same. Let me put it this way, if over time we watched fifty violent films, the plots and storylines will be different but the content is essentially the same. And that content is − violence. So, we have watched fifty films but we have fundamentally only absorbed one basic message. Furthermore, if the levels of violence within those fifty films gradually increase as each film progresses, the viewer will unwittingly have increased their capacity and tolerance of violent content. The very same principles apply to horror films or films with sexual content. By frequent, long term and habitual exposure, we gradually and unconsciously, accept more shocking or more explicit content. A fundamental problem is that we have come to 'trust' this media – and we quite simply shouldn't.

If we apply the same principle to the offering of the numerous television soaps and TV dramas that much of society follows daily, yes the actors and the storylines may be different but they almost invariably project the same message and the same image of society. An image which disproportionally depicts failed relationships, strife within families, jealousy, revenge, violence, absent fathers, rebellious, dysfunctional youngsters and general promiscuity as being the norm. The problem is that whilst we may call it 'entertainment' it does in fact instil a considerable element of 'conditioning' upon viewers and subsequently on society at large.

Remember, this book is aimed at highlighting the detrimental effects and influences from external sources on our children and young people. Today in the 21st century, as I have outlined in previous chapters, the very obvious source of that influence is the uncensored content and prolific streaming of a host of unhealthy and corrosive images, content and ideologies via television, the internet and social media and the ease of access to it. The point I am making is that strategic indoctrination and social conditioning today is the same now as it has always been. Nowadays however, due to modern technology, it is simply much more sophisticated – and considerably more influential, potent and far-reaching than it ever was before. From the story we are looking at here, in the days of Daniel, some two thousand four hundred years ago, a programme of indoctrination and conditioning was face-to-face and hands-on and took three years. You might say it was up-close and personal. Almost seventy years ago, Ray Bradbury foresaw the societal saturation potential of the then, mere two channel part-time broadcasts of the black and white television and its huge impact on society as this media continued to develop, both technologically and influentially.

We must surely urgently ask ourselves the question: Now, today, seventy years later, with all of the unfettered, unregulated and uncensored, constantly available and immediately and personally available media today – what influence is that having on our children and young people now and what affect is it going to have on them and society in the long term and into the future?

I'm only speculating now, but had Bradbury personally been optimistic about society's future in general and the development and positive use of television media in particular, he would have written a book depicting a 'utopian' future where everything was wholesome, positive and good. However, he didn't. Instead he gave us the fascinating but tragic tale of Montag and Mildred, living in a society where so much was wrong and where technologically powered mass media was being used to the detriment, not the benefit of society and to control, not liberate its citizens.

So where does the story of Daniel fit in and what can be learned from it in relation to the subject of this book? The story of Daniel is one of a clash of cultures, a clash of ideologies and a struggle between freedom and domination, liberty and dictatorship, individuality and mass conditioning.

I believe it very powerfully and profoundly demonstrates the techniques used by those who, for whatever reason, wish to impose not just their rule but also their ideology on a population. Such techniques are still very much applicable today and have been used to great effect for millennia to indoctrinate and over time, subjugate entire societies. Like Bradbury having an understanding of the world around him and that understanding informing his predictions, the writer of the book of Daniel clearly understood the propensity for people to organise themselves into societies and for some of those people to want to 'control' everyone else. But control them for what reason? So the minority can impose their ideology on the majority and do so with minimum resistance by use of specific methods and strategies.

The writer of the book of Daniel, all those years ago, evidently understood this to be one of the darker, less attractive sides of human nature. And because human beings cover the entire planet, this control element manifests in different places and at different times. It is essentially always about a specific ideology. But to instil an ideology on an entire society, or even an entire civilisation, takes strategy, organisation and the ability to influence on a large scale. Influence which is aimed at spreading – and subtly imposing that ideology. Bear in mind that quite apart from the obvious religious elements of the Bible it is also a history book spanning thousands of years of early history and traces the rise and fall of many kings, peoples, cultures, nations and empires. It is therefore a very rich and reliable source of insight and information when considering current cultures and related issues.

Don't you think it's interesting that over the years, families in TV soaps and dramas haven't become happier, solved their problems and become more functional? Violent films haven't become less violent. Overt and explicit sexual content hasn't become more moderate. Horror films haven't become more family friendly as a form of entertainment. On the contrary, throughout all of these genres there appears to be an underlying, unspoken drive to gradually and incrementally increase the 'appetite' of the viewer for more and more negative, salacious, disturbing and graphic content. That is hardly a positive, creative and helpful image and message to be continually broadcasting throughout society. Why do you suppose that is? What are the objectives? What is the endgame? Yet, at the same time we are supposed to be (according to the rhetoric of 'the news media') moving towards becoming a more enlightened, more informed, more progressive and more tolerant and inclusive society. So why doesn't the mass media machine script that into their storylines? It just doesn't make any sense.

As we read through the account of these four youngsters from all those years ago, we discover a remarkably similar situation to what we have today concerning the mass media proliferation of society. Sometime after their captivity in Babylon had begun, King Nebuchadnezzar had a giant golden statue made of himself, of his own image. It was about one hundred feet high and ten feet wide. So, it was BIG! It was bright. It shimmered and glistened. It was so big and all-pervasive; it could be seen from anywhere and everywhere in the city. Sounds familiar? It's quite literally 'in your face'. Everyone could easily see it − no matter where they were. It was an 'image' that the King wanted to 'project' and it was an image that he himself had created. Furthermore, we shall discover that the sole purpose of this giant shimmering image was that 'everyone' should look at it. It was specifically created to be the focus of everyone's attention, the subject of everyone's interest and the centre of everyone's lives. Sounds remarkably like the ever present, ubiquitous overbearing, all-pervasive influence in the 21st century of mass media via television, the internet, laptop and iPad screens, smartphones etc. to me! It doesn't matter where you go, it's there − and it demands to be looked at.

So, he had an image made, one that represented himself. An image that reflected everything that he stood for: his ideals, his morals, his values, his beliefs, his desires, his worldview and his plans and objectives. An image that conveyed, quite literally 'his image' and through which he would convey, or 'broadcast' his particular message, or ideology, to the nations. So why was Nebuchadnezzar not content with just living his life and pursuing all of his personal desires, likes, ambitions etc. and simply let everyone else do the same? The answer is quite simple − he wanted to dominate everyone else and do so by enforcing his views onto them. He was setting up a totalitarian regime: a dictatorship. One in which everyone had to look at the same object and 'take in' the same image. He wanted everyone − the whole of society, the whole of his empire to be giving attention to and focussing on the same image: an image that he had created for the sole purpose of getting everyone else to look at. Sounds a bit far-fetched that this ancient Middle Eastern Biblical event could somehow relate to 21st century technological mass media? Consider this: I have referred to Ray Bradbury's *Fahrenheit 451* as a secular prophecy because, a mere sixty-five years ago, he wrote it as a future prediction based upon his understanding of the times in which he lived, his understanding of politics and socio-political ideologies and his personal insights into human nature. And if the truth be told, he has been proven to be pretty accurate on the subject.

I see the account of Nebuchadnezzar's scheme however more as a sacred prophecy because I believe it represents more of a spiritual insight into the human condition as well as just the political, societal and technological factors that informed Bradbury. It predicts what society could become if people allow themselves to be conditioned by a bigger or higher force. The thing to bear in mind is that conditioning is not obvious, at least not in the early stages. It is subtle. The process and the programming are presented as friendly, well intended, attractive, innocent and benign. It is introduced gradually, incrementally and subliminally. As the 'heat' rises, as the ideological temperature slowly increases, we don't notice. Then, even when it gets a bit 'hot' we might notice, however, no one else seems to be bothered, so we 'collectively' think everything is okay. Remember the frog and the boiling pot from chapter one!

I think it's fair to assume that the conditioning and indoctrination process that was planned for Daniel and his friends was part and parcel of Babylonian culture under King Nebuchadnezzar. After all that clearly was the kind of person he was. He wanted to dominate. His style was totalitarian. Why else would he want to begin to indoctrinate Daniel and his friends as soon as they arrived in his kingdom? The citizens of Babylon were already conditioned through state-driven indoctrination. Daniel and his friends stood out. They would have to be conditioned if they were to fit in. Metaphorically speaking, they would have to be made to eat the same diet. It was important that they were made to be like everyone else. If you can get one hundred people to all think alike, you can control one hundred people. If you can get a thousand people to think alike, you can control that thousand people. If you can get a million people to think alike, you get my point. Expand that to a nation. Take it even further, to encompass an entire culture. Now that is indoctrination and conditioning on a grand scale. But to indoctrinate and condition the 'masses', you need 'mass methods.' Say hello to 21st century mass media. 'We have the technology!'

When it says that 'everyone' had to look at the image it is no exaggeration. What happened next is indeed remarkable and highly relevant to the subject of this book. Once the giant golden image was in place, Nebuchadnezzar then sent orders across his entire empire to make people attend the dedication of his image. However, the orders were initially to specific key people within society. It actually lists them: 'He sent orders to gather together, the princes, the governors, the captains, the judges, the treasurers, the counsellors, the sheriffs and all the rulers of the provinces, to come to the dedication of the image which Nebuchadnezzar had set up. In other words, he firstly made the requirement for everyone's attention to the image part of the key departments of the infrastructure of society. In other words he strategically ensured that his ideology was firmly embedded within the system and that there was a system in place that facilitated, supported and carried his 'vision'.

Way back then, King Nebuchadnezzar wanted to impose his 'image' on the whole of society, at least the society within his empire, and he knew how to do it. It was strategic, it was structured, it was gradual, so gradual that people didn't notice. And it was very highly organised. Mass media broadcasting in the 21st century basically follows the same principles and has precisely the same effect. However, with today's technology, it has complete global reach and influence to quite literally 'beam' any image into every nation, every country, every community and every home. And onto every device that our children and young people have access to, including those that they personally and privately carry with them and hold, quite literally, in the very palm of their hand.

Today, the world over, there are particular movements, groups and organisations, advertisers, special interest groups, pressure groups, militant organisations, political activists and so on, all seeking to convey their message and imprint their particular 'image' upon society, upon the individual and particularly upon the minds of the young and impressionable. And through 21st century mass media technology they quite literally have the means to do so to a world audience. Namely – us!

Nebuchadnezzar already had the systematic indoctrination programme in place. He already had his key people throughout his empire in place. He already had the singular, central, all-pervasive, shimmering golden image in place. He only needed one more essential ingredient to complete the potent mix. What, you may well ask was that? Simple – *music*! And lots of it.

After the gathering of the state officials to the dedication of the giant statue of the image of Nebuchadnezzar, the narrative continues: 'Then a herald cried aloud saying – To you it is commanded, all people, nations and languages, that when you hear the sound of the cornet, the flute, the harp, the sackbut, (trombone) the psaltery, (guitar) the dulcimer, (zither) and all kinds of music – you shall fall down and worship the golden image that Nebuchadnezzar the king has set up.'

It goes on to say, 'Therefore at that time when all the people heard the sound of the cornet, the flute, the harp, the sackbut, the psaltery, the dulcimer and all kinds of music, all the people, the nations and the languages, bowed down and worshipped the golden image that Nebuchadnezzar the king had set up.'

I'm sure you have already noticed that almost without exception, absolutely every TV programme is introduced with music. Every film is accompanied by music. Most adverts are accompanied by a jingle. Even national TV news now begins with a ludicrous and immensely irritating backbeat, as if the viewing public is considered unable to cope with serious stuff without a 'beat' to accompany it.

You will recall from chapter one where we considered the effects of the '60s' 'Pop' music revolution and how it carried its message throughout society then around the world. But the 'message' carried on the wings of that music also heralded in an age of radical social and ideological change. Such is the phenomenal power and influence of music. Even way back then, in the recesses of ancient history, Nebuchadnezzar clearly understood this. So much so that music – on a huge scale – was the icing on the cake of his mass media, multi-layered, nation-wide, indoctrination and conditioning propaganda programme; a literal 'programme' to reach the masses. So – together with the planned and structured, gradual, ideological 'programming' of his citizens, the strategic briefing of all state officials, the erection of the giant, all-pervasive shimmering golden image – cue the music. Let the party begin. Everybody dance now. Everyone now dance to the same tune. Be there or be square. No questions asked. Just gaze mindlessly at the image and sway to the music. After all, everyone else is doing it. It must be right. It can't be wrong. It can't do any harm. Can it?

So the entire population were commanded to bow down and worship the golden statue. The term worship, in addition to having religious connotations can also mean; to honour, to give reverence to, to give devotion to and to stand in awe of. Something that a person 'worships' therefore is also something that they hold in high regard. Something that holds high priority in their lives, something they give a lot of attention and time to. Something they look to for relevance and meaning. Something therefore that has considerable influence in their lives.

King Nebuchadnezzar wanted his giant golden image to be 'worshipped' so that he could influence, control and dominate his subjects. His strategy was to get them to look at the same object and hear the same sound, via the 'projection' of an immense golden 'shimmering' image accompanied by lots of mesmerising music. His personal propaganda therefore was carried on the wings of 'programmed sight and sound'. Welcome to the world of 'entertainment!'

Globally, today in the 21st century – TV, film, telecommunications, information technology, companies, advertisers and organisations are hell-bent on drawing everyone to their image by whatever means possible. Some just to keep selling their product, others, with the support, backing and funding from a range of propagandists, intent on promoting their particular image of politics, morality, ideology and worldview. What the general population are doing by blindly consuming all that the mass media machine is churning out 24/7 x 365 days a year, is unwittingly buying into the messages behind those images. And because it is all presented as glamorous and exciting and harmless 'entertainment' we are unaware of its pernicious, subliminal influence and its long-term effects, both on us individually and upon society at large.

You may well be thinking at this stage of reading this book that this story about Nebuchadnezzar and his giant gold statue is ancient and has no relevance today. If so, consider these few facts:

Firstly: The Academy Awards, commonly known as the Oscars, is awarded annually by the Academy of Motion Picture Arts and Sciences to recognise achievements in cinematic excellence. Winners of the award are given an 'Oscar' statuette, the highest possible award in the film industry. What does an 'Oscar' look like? Well, it is a 13.5 inches high, miniature 'gold' statuette – of a man! Yes, a miniature gold statuette of a man. Fascinating, isn't it? Oscar's design is said to depict a knight, standing on a reel of film, holding a crusaders sword. A miniature version, 'symbolically' at least, of someone else a long time ago who did it all before? Did it all before for self-aggrandisement, for power, influence, attention and dominion. If that's not quite enough, the 'man' is depicted as a knight with a sword standing on (the base) of a reel of film. This speaks fairly clearly of power and dominion, even force, or at least, coercion by 'projected' imagery and sound. Sound familiar? Also, the incorporation in its design of a knight holding a crusaders sword is also worth some thought. The last crusade was around seven hundred years ago. Why should the film industry elite adopt such ancient iconography? What is its relevance to 21st century media? Suddenly the

Nebuchadnezzar scenario perhaps doesn't seem so far-fetched or distant after all, does it?

Next: The Golden Globe Awards are accolades bestowed by the ninety-three members of the Hollywood Press Association for excellence in film and television, both domestic and abroad. Its design is also interesting. It is a 'gold' globe depicting the world. Around it is wrapped part of a reel of film. The symbolism here seems fairly clear – to encompass and influence the entire world through the medium of film?

Nebuchadnezzar's ambition was for his 'image' to be carried as far across his empire as possible by whatever means were available to him at the time. Today's technology completely circumvents the entire globe. Not only so – with the advent of the smartphone, it can now also reach, and thereby influence us, individually, personally and privately. Going back briefly, I mention that it's the ninety-three members of the Hollywood Press Association who award the Golden Globe. Consider for a moment Nebuchadnezzar's strategy of putting in place a network of key state officials within all the provinces throughout his empire, to essentially facilitate the timing, the coordination and the distribution of his mass media, image projecting, music fuelled, state orchestrated programme.

The Hollywood Press Association is part of a global support network responsible for publicising, promoting and distributing its product. It is gigantic and its sole objective is to sell, sell, sell. To sell the very latest incarnation of what they want to project to the world on that 'shimmering' screen – and all other screens, large and small. Award shows, prime-time chat show appearances by the 'Stars', billboards, forthcoming attraction bites on existing releases, showbiz magazines, celebrity magazines, tabloid coverage and finally, cinemas. Then the much anticipated drum-roll, cue the music – everybody watch now. Bow down to the latest golden image of the global mass media multi-billion dollar marketing machine. And worship the cinematography, the latest hi-tech effects, the best screenplay ever, the best screenwriter of the year, the most amazing soundtrack, actors nominated for a range of awards, surely it must win an award for artistic merit and it's already nominated for five more! But let's not for one single moment (if we have one to spare in our hectic, pressured 21st century lives) forget the glittering and glamorous 'Stars', 'Film Stars', 'Icons', and 'Idols!'. Yes, of course, they are truly all of these wonderful things, aren't they? It has been said that if you tell the people a big enough lie, loud enough and long enough, they will eventually believe it.

Finally: The Emmy Award is awarded by the Academy of Television the Arts and Sciences.

Awards are given in relation to national television broadcasts.

The Emmy statuette depicts a winged woman holding an atom (which actually looks more like the globe of the world) on outstretched arms. It is said to symbolise the Television Academy's goal of supporting and uplifting the art and science of television. The wings are said to represent the arts and the atom, the electron of science. It is yet another 'gold' statue that celebrates and rewards mass media broadcasting.

Its symbolism of a 'winged' woman is clearly intended to represent something celestial and wonderful. That's quite an image to try to sell to the world. The atom? Well, atoms as we know, are the very substance of, well – everything. The very building blocks of life itself. Talk about propaganda!

The use of ancient religious iconography (the winged woman) is again also very interesting. Such depictions of winged beings in religious literature are generally with regard to them being a celestial 'messenger'. Once again – that's quite a claim!

Celestial messengers, the building blocks of life and a single golden image for all to 'worship!' Nebuchadnezzar, Hollywood, Oscar, idols, stars and icons. A new world religion perhaps?

Yes indeed, the story of Nebuchadnezzar and his overbearing shimmering golden statue, news of which was distributed via a highly organised network and demanding everyone's focus and attention. And which was proclaimed to all his subjects throughout his empire via a cacophony of music, is all a bit far-fetched and irrelevant in the 21st century – isn't it?

But what, you might be thinking, about Daniel and his three young friends? We seem to have lost them on our journey and they are after all what this brief socio-drama is all about. To find out what happened to them and how Nebuchadnezzar's schemes affected them we have to go back to the beginning of their story. To quote a former great British statesman: 'Now this is not the end. It is not even the beginning of the end. But it is perhaps, the end of the beginning.' I truly believe, with regard to the concerns and dangers that I highlight in this book and in this chapter in particular – that it simply doesn't need to be like this. If we are prepared to take notice, take heed, take stock and take action then this is not the end, it's the beginning. The beginning of a long overdue awareness and a realisation that we as a society have allowed this multi-media technology to have gained far too much of an inroad into our daily lives and therefore have way to much influence. But just like a bad diet – we can change it. We can drastically reduce our consumption and choose rather to exercise our time and interests in much more wholesome, natural and healthy pursuits.

Before Nebuchadnezzar's plans had even had time to get off the ground, Daniel and his friends had decided they were having none of it. They knew that what would start as being seemingly innocent and harmless was going to lead to something quite different. They knew that what was being offered as being good for them would do them harm in the long term. They already liked themselves, they liked their own culture and they came from a cultural background that embraced strong community and family values. They had a strong sense of identity and they had no intention of trading or selling out those good things for something an outside influence sought to impose upon them. Their attitude was:

'It's on offer – but we don't want it.'

'It's available – but we're not interested.'

'It's free – but we still don't want it.'

'You say it's the best of stuff – but we don't care.'

'Everyone else is taking it – but it's just not for us.'

'Thanks but – no thanks.'

They refused to 'eat' the daily provision that the king appointed them. Allegorically and symbolically:

They refused to take part in what was being offered.

They refused to absorb the new culture that was being forced on them.

They refused to be assimilated.

They refused to be conditioned.

They refused to be dictated to.

They refused to play the game.

They refused to become someone and something they were not.

Here's my point: The mass media can dish all their stuff up – but we don't have to sit at the table.

We don't have to consume it.

We don't have to absorb it.

We don't have to feed on it daily.

We don't have to watch it habitually

We don't have to accept what other people dish up.

We don't have to be conditioned by it. We don't have to let it dictate to us.

When it came time to 'dance to the tune' and to worship the golden image they simply said – NO!

Thankfully, today, in the 21st century, watching television is not compulsory – yet!

Conclusion

Now that you have read this short book, my hope is that you might view that shimmering box in the corner of your living room or indeed the flickering screen on your wall, and the various other screens, in a somewhat different light. If you do then I very humbly consider myself to have done a good thing. That I have made a positive, creative, wholesome and beneficial contribution, unlike much of the content that is currently poured out through those devices.

Would we as parents allow complete strangers to come into our homes and tell our children and our families what to do, what to think and what to believe, whilst we stood idly by? Of course we wouldn't, that's preposterous. Yet that is in fact − precisely what we are allowing television and other media sources do nowadays. Of course the viewing public certainly didn't start out with that intention. We simply began during the early '50s just casually watching innocent, family friendly TV as a means of entertainment and news updates.

However, as technology has advanced we have slowly and gradually incorporated mass media in all the forms we have identified within the preceding chapters as now being an integral part of our lives, our individual psyche and our national psyche. Just like the frog in the pot of water that gradually increased in temperature. What started as the 'telly' in the corner of the family living room has grown into a 'must watch' anywhere and everywhere multi-media, screaming monster.

Even as I come to the end of writing this book, several new adverts have appeared on television. All promoting the advantages of even more programmes, more broadband, more apps and more ways to speed up and expand what is already available.

One advert depicts a father sitting at the wheel of his car in a safari park with a well-known Hollywood actor playing the part of his passenger. In the back seat are the father's two teenage children. Something terrible has happened. What is this tragedy? It's this: both teenagers complain to their father – that they have 'run out of data'. Firstly note, lest we miss the blatant portrayal of this image of the modern family – they are visiting a safari park with their father, one would assume to look at the animals. But no, the father is looking at the animals but both youngsters are in the back seat, absorbed in their smartphones. In other words – the children were with their father, but not really 'with' their father. And this image is portrayed as acceptable and normal. The fact is – for most sensible, normal families, this would not be acceptable and normal. However, if this very expensive ad is run long enough and often enough, say twenty times a day or more, every day, at prime time, for several months, on top of the advertising campaign that ran before it, also for several months, selling essentially the same product and if enough people watch it, which they will, then it will accomplish that drip-drip effect of suggestion-repetition-persuasion that I introduced in the first chapter of this book.

The 'concerned' father responds by saying: 'What can I do? I can hardly give you some of my data.' Wait a minute… can't these teenagers survive an hour or so until they get home without data for their phones? According to this awful EE Communications advert, apparently not. But the passenger chirps in: 'But Dad, yes you can. You can make your kids happy. With this new app, you can now 'gift' your data to your kids!'

What? Yes, this wonderful father, distressed because his grown up children apparently can't survive for five minutes without their smartphones can now immediately use this amazing new app to transfer data from his phone to theirs – as a 'gift!' Now, the advertisers would have us believe, everyone is happy again.

A new BT TV advert is promoting 'BT Superfast Fibre Essential'. The word to watch here is the word 'essential'. Yes, they want you and me and indeed everyone to believe this product is − essential. That, by implication, is you simply can't live without it. What utter nonsense! The very same product was previously peddled as BT Infinity. The simple fact is that these mass media multinational global corporations unashamedly sell their products as if it was washing powder. Add a blue speck to the same old but call it something different.

Quite unbelievably that same advert concludes with 'This is not fantasy − this is reality'.

And 'BT − be there'. So − they are now peddling fantasy − as reality. But blatantly telling us − this is not fantasy, its reality! And 'Be There'. Be where exactly? Beware. Oh beware. Now I've got it!

And yet another one: 'Now TV' promoting their new Smart-Stick Bundle, boast that by inserting their smart-stick into the back of your TV you can now access 'thousands more programmes and hundreds of box sets, free and without a contract'. Exactly what we all need to live a fuller, more satisfying, meaningful and rewarding life. Thousands more programmes and hundreds more box sets, i.e. a few thousand even more, utterly time wasting, life wasting, mind numbing, energy sapping viewing hours, of goodness knows what? Incredibly, this particular ad concludes with the statement: 'This is an offer you simply cannot afford to miss.'

Again, take note of the 'directive' around these promotions: 'Essential', 'Must Have', 'You cannot afford to miss'. Doesn't that remind you of Nebuchadnezzar's Golden Image? The comparison is unavoidable: Look at it. You must look at it. Everyone must look at it. Also, like the Nebuchadnezzar story, there is a relentless drive to feed the entire population the same diet; a visual diet, a cultural diet and an ideological diet.

This book is actually a good bit longer than I had originally intended it to be. I thought it was finished when I wrote chapter one. I saw it as a booklet, designed as a short sharp read. An alert and a call to action. Although I personally held a lot more views on the subject, I felt that what is now chapter one, was sufficient. The publishers however thought otherwise and encouraged me to write more, to expand on the subject. I'm glad they did. I had been impacted for some time about the profoundly lucid relevance of *Fahrenheit 451* and the Biblical account of Daniel and Nebuchadnezzar as well as other pieces of classic 'prophetic' literature such as George Orwell's *1984* and Aldous Huxley's *Brave New World*. These works and others like them are prophetic voices from the past, wisely alerting us to dangers in the future. That future is – NOW. If we choose to ignore those warnings, we do so at our peril. If however, we take notice and learn from them, we can make changes, alter course and avert disaster.

Another thing I want to mention is that in this book, I don't address the issues around video games and whatever else they might also be called these days. The reasons are because I simply don't know enough about them, particularly because the technology around them advances at an alarming rate, as does the terminology. But also because they are just another expression of the problem that society now has with 'screens' spewing out images and 'messages' through such devices.

What I do know is that many parents have considerable difficulty controlling their children's use of them as well as being very concerned about the graphic violence and other content associated with these, so-called 'games'.

I also intentionally don't attempt to look at 'what's next?' I am aware however that three-dimensional imagery via smartphones is already with us in fairly rudimentary form – for now. 'Sensory Imagery' will become widely available. This involves somehow 'feeling' what you are seeing. 'Interactive' games and programmes via Xbox and such like will continue to be developed. Commercial access to 'Hologram' technology is not too far away. Again – these are remarkable technologies with huge potential for the benefits of society. But will they be marketed for the right reasons? Will they be utilised for the right reasons?

What is a real and present danger is this: That our children and young people are growing up in a society where 'virtual reality' is being promoted and sold as having more to offer and as having greater meaning and greater significance – than 'actual' reality. Exaggeration? Alarmist? Think about the BT advert claiming 'this is not fantasy, this is reality'. Remember Bradbury's Mildred, whose only 'real' family was the talking walls. Many official statistics already reveal that a disproportionate and unprecedented number of children and young people across the wide spectrum of society feel disconnected, isolated, confused and depressed; resulting in, among other treatments, a significant increase in their use of anti-depressant medication. We must urgently ask ourselves – just how does this correlate to their constant exposure to mass media and their addictive use of social media in all its forms?

We have instant contacts, instant communication, instant friends, instant images, instant information, instant programmes, instant films, instant entertainment, instant music and instant gratification. Just gaze at the golden image and dance to the music. But the tragic cry of so many young lives must surely be – but what does this all mean? What's it all about? Where am I going? What should I be doing? What is actually 'real?'

End

Bibliography

1. (Source: Gareth Rose and Kay Smith. 'Pornography awareness lessons' for kids as young as 10. The Mail on Sunday, July 15th 2018)

2. (Source: Children with gender doubts 'often have trans friends'. By Victoria Allen, Science Correspondent, Daily Mail August 24th 2018)

3. (Source: References made to Fahrenheit 451, adapted from Fahrenheit 451 by Ray Bradbury. Harper Collins Publishers)

4. (Source: Adapted from national UK mainstream television adverts by BT, EE, Now TV – Broadcast during 2018)